MW00588480

PARTICIPANT
JOURNAL **TWO**

SEASONS OF HOPE

M. Donna MacLeod

AVE MARIA PRESS AVE Notre Dame, Indiana

To Erynne Lee MacLeod,

a cherished child

who loved Jesus

and now lives with him.

Scripture quotations contained herein are from the *New Revised Standard Version* of the Bible, copyright © 1993 and 1989, by the Division of Christian Education of the National Council of the Churches of Christ in the U.S.A., and are used by permission. All rights reserved.

Quotations from the English translation of the *Catechism of the Catholic Church* for the United States of America, copyright © 1994, United States Catholic Conference, Inc.—*Libreria Editrice Vaticana* are used by permission.

Founded in 1865, Ave Maria Press is a ministry of the United States Province of Holy Cross.

www.avemariapress.com

ISBN-10 1-59471-113-5   ISBN-13 978-1-59471-113-8

Cover and text design by John Carson.

Printed and bound in the United States of America.

Contents

"Seasons of Hope Prayer"

Our Father,
in this season of sorrow,
we turn to you.
Weakened with sadness,
we shed tears beyond number.
May those you send to help us
bring your love and consolation.

In this season of sorrow,
we lift up our broken hearts to you.
Heal us with your tender mercy and
make this a season of hope.
Trusting in your infinite kindness,
we ask this of you
with the Son and the Holy Spirit.
Amen.

Welcome to the

Participant Journal

Dear Brothers and Sisters in Christ Jesus,

When your loved one went home to the Lord, did you think that God was calling you to a new life in him, too? And that this new life held much more than pain and sorrow?

I had no idea what lay ahead when my daughter Erynne died. Years of caring for the dying and their families as a nurse did not prepare me for my own grief. Yet God would use the lessons I learned for the good of others. From the loss of a precious child a Christ-centered ministry to the bereaved and a hospice were born. God plans ahead. He didn't forget me, my family, or my community, and he hasn't forgotten you. He wants to console you.

Trusting in God and coming to the *Seasons of Hope* program blesses you in untold ways. The support of others who know what you go through is the first of many of God's gifts of love. Your broken heart will mend as your spirit lifts. I've seen it happen time and again.

A bible and this *Participant Journal* are all you need for the group sessions of *Seasons of Hope*. A group prayer begins the booklet and each session. Each week the facilitator will have you open to the Guidepost page for the theme, scripture citation, and activity to do before faith sharing begins.

The rest of the weekly journal is for you to use at home after the session. It generally takes about twenty minutes to complete the weekly homework—a commitment that most schedules can handle. If possible, find a quiet corner that is free of distractions. A good way to get focused is to read the week's Bible passage.

The opening comments in Looking Back give a fresh way to view the scripture story. The spiritual journey that began in the group session continues as you ask for guidance with A Prayer to Find the Way. You will read Steps Along the Path to learn how the scripture story relates to mourning and then spend time with the Reflection section to consider your situation. You can write your thoughts in the space provided under the heading, Journal Entry.

To help you cope, Moving Forward offers a Church tradition or an act of charity that generates hope. You finish the weekly journey with the Closing Prayer thanking God for the gift of consolation.

The end of the booklet has treasures of its own. Are you interested in literature and Web sites about losing a loved one? Check out Helpful Resources. Need a place to record contact information about your new friends at *Seasons of Hope*? Use the Network Directory. How about ground rules for the group? That's covered in Guide to Group Etiquette. Want to help your facilitators plan for the next season? The Season Two Survey lets you formally share your ideas.

With *Participant Journal* homework, you privately bring the trials of your loss to the Lord. You embrace his teachings, reflect on your loss, and share the painful moments so that your wounded spirit can grow strong in Christ.

May this unique way of placing Jesus Christ at the center of your grief bring you consolation.

In Christ,

M. Donna MacLeod

Session ONE

Guidepost: Point of Departure

Theme of the first session:

Remembering

Scripture: Luke 24:1–12

🍃 Marking the Route

Exercise:

In the cluster group, focus on your first experiences with wakes and funerals by completing these statements:

- My name is _____.

- What I remember most about wakes and funerals when I was a child is . . .

- The thing my parent(s) did that most impressed me is . . .

- The part God played in what I remember is . . .

Notes

Home Journal: Point of Departure

Looking Back: *Disbelief*

This week in the group session we heard the passage from Luke 24:1–12 in which the women at the empty tomb needed angels to remind them of Jesus' promise of resurrection. Losing a loved one numbs those who are left behind and sometimes even shakes the faith of the devout. Jesus had spoken openly about his impending death and God's plan that he would rise again; yet, none of his closest friends understood.

Losing a loved one gives us insight into how distressed the disciples were. Early on, we might have a hard time believing that a loved one is gone. We may even wonder about what happens to a soul in the afterlife.

The women at the tomb benefited from messengers of God who assured them that Jesus lived on. Most of us aren't enlightened by heavenly messengers when a death occurs, but God has other means. What about the people who reach out to us with words of consolation about Jesus' promise of everlasting life? Also consider how the Church shares God's message of love through the wake and funeral services, and the *Seasons of Hope* ministry. Have these acts of compassion bolstered your faith in God?

A Prayer to Find the Way

O divine Savior,
you are with me in my moments
of believing and questioning.
You know how much I long
to be faithful to you.
When darkness enters my thoughts
about losing my loved one,
let your spirit of wisdom
brighten my path.
Help me understand
and embrace your message.
Amen.

Steps Along the Path

Jesus always knew where his followers were on their spiritual journeys. The women at the tomb believed in him and salvation, but became confused when confronted by death. The apostles seemed to have a crisis of faith. Jesus, however, remained a faithful guide and teacher. He never gave up on them even in their darkest moments. When you open your grief to his tender care, you too can expect to grow spiritually.

Reflection

Find a memento of your deceased loved one that brings back memories of a happier time. Hold it in your hands and savor the positive feelings you once experienced with that person.

Journal Entry

Think about how mourning the loss of your loved one has affected your relationship with the Lord.

Are you as confused as the women staring at the burial cloths in the empty tomb?

Do you believe you will never be happy again?

Has grief hindered your prayer and worship?

Are you disinterested like the apostles who considered the women's story nonsense?

Or do you find yourself clinging to the Lord?

Whatever spiritual state you're in, it helps to write to Jesus about your reaction to losing a loved one. The act of writing can move emotions from inside you to the paper. It gives you something tangible. Often you can write words that are difficult to speak.

If you need a little help, try one of these opening phrases:

Since _____died, I. . .

Lord, I'm having trouble believing that. . .

Moving Forward

Prayer wasn't mentioned in the passage from Luke, but the women who went to attend to the body would have prepared for the sacred task by praying. On the way to the tomb, some were probably praying for the courage to face a world without their beloved Jesus.

Do your petitions to God seek courage? Prayer is inspired by God's grace, and that same grace can help you decide what to pray for. God wants you to trust in him, to trust that he hasn't forgotten your loved one. He doesn't want you to forget your loved one either. Praying for the soul of the deceased is a powerful way to respond.

Consider offering a prayer as you place a memento of your loved one by his or her picture.

Closing Prayer

Almighty God,
let the grace of this time with you
refresh my heart and soul.
Help me to better understand
my reaction to losing my loved one.
Grant this through Christ our Lord.
Amen.

Session TWO

Guidepost: Path to Understanding

Theme of the second session:

Seeking Consolation

Scripture: John 5:1–9

 Marking the Route

Exercise:

One way to focus on Jesus during mourning is to write to him about what seems to cripple you spiritually. In the space provided below, let him know whether you are ready to pick up the pieces of your life.

Notes

Home Journal: Path to Understanding

Looking Back: *Seeking Consolation*

People believed that an angel of the Lord came down into the pool of Bethesda every so often and stirred it up. Whoever was first to get in after it was stirred was healed of his or her infirmity. The crippled man we encountered in John 5:1–9 positioned himself at the pool to be cured, yet he never reached the healing waters in time. Perhaps he was so downhearted that he had given up. He offered excuses to Jesus, but he didn't seek healing from him. Jesus healed him anyway.

Those of us who grieve over a loved one sometimes forget to ask for God's help, too.

A Prayer to Find the Way

O divine Savior,
you are with me
in my moments of questioning.
You know how much I long
to be faithful to you.
When darkness enters my thoughts
about losing my loved one,
let your spirit of wisdom shine on
my path.
Amen.

 Steps Along the Path

Have you already found a path to healing waters that could "cure" your sorrow? Are you patiently waiting for grief to lessen? Is consolation still out of reach? Take heart. Many have traveled the same route and can testify that one day life will get better.

Grieving, though, can disable you when you practice your faith, even when you feel close to the Lord. Experiencing the pain of loss is important: it is essential grief work. You may get stuck in sadness for a while, but please be patient with yourself. Jesus understands grief, and he wants to console you.

Reflection

Conjure up an image of a pool of water, a lake, or a quiet stream that you enjoy. Pretend that you are sitting on a mat before it, contemplating your life after losing your loved one. If ripples of healing were on the water in the imagery, could you rush forth? Would anyone be there to help you? Would you invite Jesus to help you?

Journal Entry

To understand grief, it is wise to reflect on how you handle what happens in your life. Initially, losing a loved one can make the events around you blur together. You may feel like you're in a fog, detached from reality. You may even disconnect from your feelings, your behavior, and how you interact with others. If you get stalled in this phase, you might not realize that you aren't moving forward.

Write about what would help you get back on the path of life. Tell the Lord about the pain grieving brings. Let him know you want to be well. If you are doing well, give him thanks in writing.

Moving Forward

The crippled man in the scripture story claimed that no one was there to help him at the pool. He had had his infirmity for many years, and you can only wonder if his defeatist attitude distanced his friends and family.

Although grief makes it hard to be cheerful, faith can help you hope in the future. Acts of consolation make a connection with the soul of both the giver and the receiver. If you failed to acknowledge such a gesture, express thanks to the person now. Offer God a prayer of gratitude for the gifts of love he sends your way during mourning.

Closing Prayer

O Jesus,
may your consolation
and spirit of love
reach the inner recesses
of my broken heart.
Let me accept your healing power
and rise from the mat of my grief
to walk with you this week.
I ask the Father this in your name.
Amen.

Session THREE

Guidepost: Obstacles on the Journey

Theme of the third session:

Stumbling Blocks

Scripture: Isaiah 57:14–15

🍃 Marking the Route

Exercise:

Pick a stone that represents a stumbling block you currently face on the path to healing. Notice the size, color, shape, and texture of your selection.

In the space below write to Jesus to:

- describe your "real" stumbling block.

- explain what the stone you selected tells you about your loss.

Notes

Home Journal: Obstacles on the Journey

Looking Back: *Stones For Building*

Most of us consider grieving a major stumbling block to happiness. Yet this week's passage from Isaiah 57:14–15 reveals that God wants every obstruction to be removed from our path. In fact, the prophet begins by telling us to build up and prepare the way.

When your heart is broken, you may feel confused about where the future will lead you. Yet Isaiah reveals that the Holy One on high is with you even when you feel devastated. God does not simply stop by for a minute; he dwells with you and wants to revive your spirit as well as your heart.

In the midst of your pain, particularly when those special events come along that stir up emotions, it can be difficult to remember that God is in this with you. If the stumbling blocks of grief wall up your heart to protect you from hurting, the loneliness of mourning can get worse. Ask for God's help, and the stumbling blocks can become a way to build a bridge to new life in him.

A Prayer to Find the Way

O dear Jesus,
you encountered stumbling blocks
on your journey among us.
Your trust in God the Father
and acceptance of his will
gives a perfect example for my trials.
As I stumble through mourning,
help me to remember
that you are by my side.
Give me the strength I need.
Amen.

Steps Along the Path

We learn in the New Testament that Jesus sought to build up his Father's kingdom. Simon, whom Jesus called Peter (derived from an Aramaic word that means "rock"), and the other apostles would become the foundation stones of the Church. Their mission to witness to Jesus as the Messiah, the Son of the living God, would establish the faith community and the oral traditions that became the gospels.

Depending on your state of mind after your loss, Jesus may be a major stumbling block for you to deal with. Perhaps you trusted him to pull your beloved from the brink of death. Maybe the person suffered. Maybe you weren't given a chance to say good-bye. When something happens that can't be reconciled with what you expect from a loving and merciful God, you may feel angry, abandoned, confused, or a host of other emotions that are all normal reactions to grieving. You might even question your beliefs.

Jesus understands your feelings. He suffered losses in his life, too. When you turn to him, the Rock of Salvation, you build up God's kingdom. Your stumbling blocks of grief are transformed into stepping-stones to God.

Reflection

How far have you come after losing a loved one? Has grieving taken you to unfamiliar territory? Life probably resembles its former state, yet its twists and turns may bring issues that need attention. Think about a boulder of a problem that you have encountered. Did it keep you from moving on?

Journal Entry

With this week's scripture in mind, write to Jesus about the state your spirit is in. If you need a little help, gaze at the stone you selected and compare its qualities with the sturdiness of your spirit.

 Moving Forward

Losing a loved one is something no one wants to encounter, yet death is part of the human experience. From it new insight into your relationship with the Lord can emerge, bringing you to an important phase of healing. When you are open to his ways, you can sense his constant love for you.

This week bless the stone you selected in session by tracing the Sign of the Cross on it. Carry it with you as a reminder of the obstacles you have overcome through the power of God's love.

Closing Prayer

O Jesus,
through you anything is possible.
May the obstacles I face
on the path of mourning
become as small as the stone I bless
this week.
I ask in your name.
Amen.

Session FOUR

Guidepost: Path to Inner Healing

Theme of the fourth session:

Living Hope

Scripture: 1 Peter 1:3–9

Marking the Route

Exercise:

Write a note of thanks to Jesus for taking your "grief."

Note: Please bring your rosary beads to group next week.

Notes

Home Journal: Path to Inner Healing

Looking Back: *Living Hope*

Scripture from the First Letter of Peter assures us that God the Father is full of mercy. The resurrection of Jesus gives his followers (even those who have not seen him) a new birth to a living hope and an inheritance in heaven.

Today some believers take salvation for granted, yet the passage reveals that when the apostles lived among new believers, faith in Jesus Christ was considered more precious than gold. The early Church leaders, however, still found it necessary to encourage hope in Jesus during difficult periods and to remind the faithful of the promise of heaven.

The Bible describes heaven in a variety of ways; for example, it calls it the blue firmament—a region of clouds that pass along the sky; and as the dwelling place of God, his angels, and the souls of the just. Saints and scholars have offered learned opinions on heaven down through the ages, and each of us has a notion of what heaven will be like.

During mourning, you may spend precious energy wondering if your loved one made it "home to God" safely. The Church assures us, "Those who die in God's grace and friendship and are perfectly purified live forever with Christ" (CCC 1023). It recognizes that everyone may not reach perfection in this life and won't be ready to live forever with Christ. These souls enter purgatory until such time that all their sins are reconciled. United with the souls in purgatory in the great communion of saints, we continue to pray for them.

The Church also teaches, "We cannot be united with God unless we freely choose to love him. But we cannot love God if we sin gravely against him, against our neighbor, or against ourselves . . ." (CCC 1033). Only God knows when someone dies without repenting and chooses to remain separate from him and the blessed.

Sometimes you just know in your heart that your loved one is with the Lord. What a blessing that is! It shows living hope that flows from the Holy Spirit.

A Prayer to Find the Way

O merciful Jesus,
you gave us living hope
through your resurrection from the
dead.
Although I have not seen you,
I love you
and trust that you
will use my sorrow
for the good of my soul.
Help me find my way.
Amen.

Steps Along the Path

The Church teaches that salvation comes from God alone. For those who keep the faith, belief in salvation straightens the winding path of mourning.

Peter's letter is meant to console when it says that disciples may have to suffer various trials for a little while. You know that "a little while" can become an eternity during sorrow. Seeking the Lord's consolation through prayer is a sure-fire way to cope in times of need.

Reflection

At the crucifixion, what disciple thought that good would come from Jesus' death? Apparently, it took time for the reality of Jesus' destiny to sink in even though he had clearly explained the meaning of his life on numerous occasions. History shows that his death and resurrection changed the world in an awesome way.

Think about your own loss. Try to find something good that has come from your loved one's death. If you can't, what would you wish for?

Journal Entry

The *Seasons of Hope* program is centered on Jesus. What you do at sessions and at home with this booklet can bring you his consolation. When you hope in Jesus, mourning takes on new meaning. Recall when you welcomed him into your grief and write about the effect that had on you.

Moving Forward

Sometimes grief makes believers feel they are losing hope. Fortunately, Jesus understands the devastating effects of grief and sorrow. A silver lining may be sewn into the darkest moments: suffering can help you understand the pain of others who grieve.

This week, focus on someone else's pain. It could be a bereaved person or someone who has lost a job or good health or faces another crisis. Make an attempt to contact him or her. Be a sign of hope.

Closing Prayer

O my Savior,
thank you for the good you bring
to my life—even in sorrow.
I am eternally grateful
for all you give me.
Amen.

Session FIVE

Guidepost: Way of Suffering

Theme of the fifth session:

The Cross

Scripture: Luke 9:22–24

Marking the Route

Exercise:

Use your rosary beads in the group this week to contemplate the cross of Christ and reflect on the suffering of our Lord and Savior. If you like, jot down your thoughts.

Note: Next week, please bring an item to show the group that reminds you of your departed loved one.

Notes

Home Journal: Way of Suffering

Looking Back: *Sorrow*

I n Luke 9:22–24, Jesus foretold his passion and death. Imagine the sorrow his mother Mary, the greatest disciple, must have felt upon hearing those words. From the time of Jesus' infancy when she and Joseph presented him in The Temple, Mary had been aware of her son's destiny. Simeon had prophesied on that day, saying, "This child is destined for the falling and rising of many in Israel, and to be a sign that will be opposed . . . " (Lk 2:34). Perhaps sorrow was always lurking in the shadows for Mary.

Only the Gospel of John mentions Jesus' mother at the foot of the cross at Golgatha, but the faithful believe that Mary was with Jesus every step of the way sharing in his suffering. Over the centuries, the Church developed themes of Mary's sorrow based on history, scripture, and legend. A special devotion known as "The Seven Sorrows of Mary" includes a meeting of Jesus and Mary on the way to his crucifixion.

We can also picture an encounter of son and mother on the way to Calvary as we pray the fourth Sorrowful Mystery of the rosary, The Carrying of the Cross. Among all of humanity, no one knew Jesus as well as Mary. Who could better lead us to the profound mystery of his life and suffering?

A Prayer to Find the Way

O suffering Savior,
you carried your cross
without complaint
and gave us eternal life.
Although my sorrow
is a heavy cross to bear,
your mercy is infinite.
Let me discover,
as did your ever-faithful mother
Mary,
the blessing hidden among the tears.
Amen.

Steps Along the Path

Jesus knew that those who choose to follow him would have suffering and sorrow at points in their lives. He embraced suffering in a way that perhaps only the saints among us can truly fathom.

We can only imagine how he might have felt on the way to Calvary when he saw the anguish in his mother's eyes. His concern for her mirrors his loving concern for the new humanity created by his redemptive act. In these difficult days of mourning, it helps to remember that you are a recipient of his loving concern.

Reflection

Mourning tends to draw even the most devout person inward. Your thoughts may center on the departed loved one, but the pain you experience is essentially that—your pain. Many of us feel that no one else can possibly understand what we are going through, yet Jesus gave his sorrowful mother to all of us. She understands.

Spend time reflecting on her sorrow as her beloved Jesus passed by on the way to Calvary. What might you ask her about sorrow? What would she tell you?

Journal Entry

When you truly encounter the Blessed Mother, you discover that she brings you to Jesus. Write to him now and share your distress, sadness, or regret over losing your loved one.

🍃 **Moving Forward**

For centuries, Catholics have contemplated the face of Christ by turning to the rosary. The repetition of Hail Marys brings forth praise of Christ. This week pray the Sorrowful Mysteries to unite your sorrow to the sorrow of the ages. Walk the spiritual road to Golgatha with the Blessed Mother and the Lord, and receive consolation.

The Sorrowful Mysteries

> *The Agony in the Garden*
> *The Scourging at the Pillar*
> *The Crowning of Thorns*
> *The Carrying of the Cross*
> *The Crucifixion*

*A brief guide, *How to Pray the Rosary*, is available online at www.avemariapress.com

Closing Prayer

O Jesus,
I lift up my sorrow to you
knowing that you are compassion
incarnate.
As I walk this path of sadness,
I am grateful that you
and Mother Mary
are at my side.
Amen.

Session SIX

Guidepost: Final Destination

Theme of the sixth session:

Do Not Be Afraid

Scripture: Luke 8:40–42, 49–56

Marking the Route

Exercise:

You will show something that reminds you of your loved one and tell why it is special to you.

Seasons of Hope has four different seasons. Find out when the next one starts.

Notes

Home Journal: Final Destination

Looking Back: *Just Have Faith*

The account in Luke 8:40–42, 49–56 this week gives valuable insight into Jesus' interest in families who lose a loved one. Jairus, the father of a dying girl, was an official of the synagogue—a position that suggests he was a devout Jew. When he beseeched Jesus by falling at his feet and begging, his belief in Jesus' healing power was demonstrated to the crowd and to the rest of us throughout the ages.

Without hesitation, Jesus went with Jairus and worked his way through crowds of people who almost crushed him. No doubt each of them wanted the Lord's undivided attention—as do we when we have pressing needs.

Someone arrived to tell Jairus not to bother Jesus any further because the girl had died. How grief stricken Jairus must have been! Yet Jesus consoled him, telling him not to be afraid, to have faith and his daughter would be saved.

Sometimes grieving can make us feel that a broken heart is beyond saving. Yet, Jesus never abandons anyone. Have you lifted up your fears to him lately?

A Prayer to Find the Way

O Jesus, healer of us all,
you knew what was best
for my loved one
when her (his) time was over.
You know how to heal
the pain of mourning, too.
Please, show me how
to let go of my fears
and walk with you.
Amen.

Steps Along the Path

It is wise to have faith in God, but losing a loved one can test even the wisest among us. We cannot create faith. It is a gift of the Holy Spirit that gives us an internal conviction that God will act on our behalf.

When you suffer through difficult trials, you have an opportunity to learn how deep your faith is. In a sense, you get a glimpse at the health of your soul.

In the scripture story, Jesus knew that Jairus was a man of faith. Jairus would not have sought his help otherwise. When they arrived at the house, it seems that Jairus (along with his wife and the disciples) wept and ridiculed Jesus because it was too much to believe that the girl was asleep as he had said. Grief had overwhelmed them.

Their shaky faith didn't stop Jesus that day. He reached out to the girl and spoke to her. She was saved as Jesus had

promised. In dark moments, try to remember that the Lord keeps his promises whether our faith is strong or shaky.

Reflection

Your journey with the Lord began long before you lost your loved one. No matter what connection you had to the deceased, you probably brought him or her to Jesus in prayer over the years. What did you say or do to bring Jesus' comfort to your suffering loved one? What did others do?

Journal Entry

We can never praise, glorify, or thank God enough for the gift of loved ones. So write to Jesus about how your departed loved one blessed your life and why you are grateful to have known him or her.

Moving Forward

To thank God for your loved one this week, consider kneeling before the tabernacle to pray. Our Church is a communion of all the faithful of Christ—those on Earth, the dead who are being purified, and the blessed in heaven. So while you are at the tabernacle, offer a few words of thanks to your departed loved one.

Closing Prayer

O Jesus,
steadfast friend of those in need
of rising to new life,
I know that you don't want me to
fear the future you have planned
for me. I trust in you.
Amen.

Appendix

Helpful Resources

BOOKS

Chatman, Delle, and William Kenneally. *The Death of a Parent: Reflections for Adults Mourning the Loss of a Father or Mother.* Chicago: ACTA, 2001.

Chilson, Richard. *Prayer: Exploring a Great Spiritual Practice.* Notre Dame, IN: Ave Maria, 2006.

Curry, Cathleen. *When Your Spouse Dies.* Notre Dame, IN: Ave Maria, 1990.

Dawson, Ann. *A Season of Grief: A Comforting Companion for Difficult Days.* Notre Dame, IN: Ave Maria, 2002.

Felber, Marta. *Finding Your Way After Your Spouse Dies.* Notre Dame, IN: Ave Maria, 2000.

Gilbert, Richard B. *Finding Your Way After Your Parent Dies: Hope for Grieving Adults.* Notre Dame, IN: Ave Maria, 1999.

Guntzelman, Joan. *God Knows You're Grieving: Things to Do to Help You Through.* Notre Dame, IN: Ave Maria, 2001.

Hamma, Robert M. *In Times of Grieving: Prayers of Comfort and Consolation.* Notre Dame, IN: Ave Maria, 2004.

Hickman, Martha Whitmore. *Healing After Loss: Daily Meditations for Working Through Grief.* New York: Avon Books, 1994.

Huntley, Theresa M. *Helping Children Grieve: When Someone They Love Dies.* Minneapolis: Augsburg Fortress, 2002.

Lafser, Christine O'Keeffe. *An Empty Cradle, A Full Heart: Reflections for Mothers and Fathers After Miscarriage, Stillbirth or Infant Death.* Chicago: Loyola Press, 1998.

Lambin, Helen Reichert. *The Death of a Husband: Reflections for a Grieving Wife.* Chicago: ACTA, 1999.

O'Brien, Mauryeen. *Lift Up Your Hearts: Meditations for Those Who Mourn.* Chicago: ACTA, 2000.

Rupp, Joyce. *Praying Our Goodbyes.* Notre Dame, IN: Ave Maria, 1988.

—————. *The Cup of Our Life: A Guide for Spiritual Growth.* Notre Dame, IN: Ave Maria, 1997.

—————. *Your Sorrow Is My Sorrow: Hope and Strength in Times of Suffering.* New York: Crossroad, 1999.

Stillwell, Elaine. *The Death of a Child: Reflections for Grieving Parents.* Chicago: ACTA, 2004.

Vogt, Robert. *The Death of a Wife: Reflections for a Grieving Husband.* Chicago: ACTA, 1997.

Wezeman, Phyllis Vos, and Kenneth R. Wezeman. *Finding Your Way After Your Child Dies.* Notre Dame, IN: Ave Maria, 2001.

Woods, Margolyn, and Maureen MacLellan. *Comfort for the Grieving Heart.* Notre Dame, IN: Ave Maria, 2002.

Zonnebelt-Smeege, Susan J., and Robert De Vries. *Getting to the Other Side of Grief: Overcoming the Loss of a Spouse.* Grand Rapids, MI: Baker Books, 1998.

WEB SITES

www.aarp.org/families/grief_loss/ has basic grief information from the AARP, 601 E St., Washington, DC 20049. 888-687-2277.

www.avemariapress.com has books on prayer, bereavement, and spiritual enrichment that comfort the downhearted.

www.bereavementmag.com connects to *Living With Loss Magazine: Hope and Healing for the Body, Mind, and Spirit.*

www.compassionatefriends.com has information and support for families who lose a child.

www.grieflossrecovery.com is a support site with related links.

www.griefwork.org offers pamphlets, books, videos, links to resources, and information on the National Catholic Ministry to the Bereaved, PO Box 16353, St. Louis, MO, 63125. 314-638-2638.

www.griefsong.com has unique ways to honor the death of a loved one.

www.widownet.com has information and self-help resources for, and by, widows and widowers.

Network Directory

Interacting with others of faith who understand what it means to lose a loved one gives you a chance to give and receive support. Use the space below for contact information of participants in your *Seasons of Hope* group.

Name_____

Phone Number_____

E-mail_____

Name_____

Phone Number_____

E-mail_____

Name_____

Phone Number_____

E-mail_____

Name_____

Phone Number_____

E-mail_____

Name_____

Phone Number_____

E-mail_____

Name_____

Phone Number_____

E-mail_____

Name_____

Phone Number_____

E-mail_____

Guide to Group Etiquette

A facilitator guides the faith sharing process by keeping the focus on the Lord and the questions. A facilitator doesn't teach, preach, or advise. He or she creates a safe place for you to talk about your feelings about loss and receive consolation.

You are expected to:

- come each week and make it known if you can't

- arrive on time

- treat others with respect

- share your faith story and then let others talk

- be a good listener

- keep what is shared in confidence

- be open to God touching you through others

Don't worry if tears flow. They are part of grieving. Smiles and laughter are welcome, too.